A Child Looking for Love

By

Tessa Marie (Grisham) Willhite

Volume One

Just like black ice, if you are not careful you can slip, slide or fall. As the snow becomes whiter and whiter, the earth begins to be covered as a blanket, as though all life becomes still.

Volume One

Preface

Throughout my life I have had to move and stay with others which has seemed like an entire life span. When my husband decided that he wanted to sell our home for the fifth time, I was devastated.

I was devastated to the point I moved to Dickson, Tennessee with my best friend and I had come to the conclusion that I was ending our marriage, since I had asked him to be with me and he would not because of the drive.

My mind began to think he did not love me because he did not want to be with me. I felt it was just like my Dad, I am not good enough, and even my Dad did not love me enough to be with me.

This is the way I thought my entire life.

No one loves me because, no one cares because, not knowing that all of my actions reflected back on my past with my Dad.

Volume One

This is where my journey began, with a pencil and paper writing down everything that was a distress to me in the way I had grown up without my Dad and how I felt.

I am dedicating my books to my friend, Liz (Elizabeth Sievers). She left to be with the Lord on September 2, 2013.

She knew everything that the Lord knew about me. She would encourage me to hold my head up high and that I was just as good as anyone else. She would tell me that if I did not know it, act like I did and move on.

Every day I would sit in her sun room and type up what I had written throughout the night. I would wake up at all hours of the night and think of different things that had been hidden way back in the deepest recesses of my mind which I held inside for all these years... events and episodes that I pushed way deep out of site.

I would keep my pencil and paper on the table next to my bed and when I woke up I would grab hold of the pencil and paper and start writing down everything that would show in the vision of my thoughts.

Volume One

During this time I had been laid off after several years of employment and had no idea what I wanted to do with myself. What did I want to do when I grew up, again?

I had my own bedroom, along with a sun room and a studio where I would spend a whole lot of time since most of the time I was alone.

Liz worked a full time shift and sometimes would not come in until later in the evening so I had a lot of time on my hands.

Alone, discouraged, and deeply depressed. There were days I just wanted to go home with the Lord and leave all this behind. I know that so many have felt like I did but, at the time, I thought I was the only one in the world who thought this way.

Liz would sit on the edge of my bed and tell me that I had to shake this off and start living again. She would tell me that she wanted her friend back.

Along with my Liz coaching me and giving me so much encouragement, telling me that we have to keep the Lord first, and changing the discouraged mind I had developed in so little time.

When it comes to the Lord's timing...

Volume One

A light began to flourish from the deep dark tunnel that was imbedded so far, not only in my mind, but my heart.

I had developed a calloused heart and soul. This was not the Tessa that I wanted to be.

I had to make the choice, and through Jesus Christ waking me up all those nights, giving me what I needed to write this book, so I could release all the anger and hate that I have felt all these years.

I miss my Liz and know she is dancing around smiling and keeping her eyes on me.

This first Book **"A Child Looking for Love"** took (2) two years to complete with a lot of prayer and I am working on my second Book **"A Crying Heart"**.

Note: We are never without a Father...
    We just have to know to look-up...

This life is yours take the power to choose what you want to do and do it well.

One night Liz had gone out of town and it was raining and storming. I remember waking up and could not raise my head as though I was being held down by a force greater than me. I was yelling for my mother at first as though I was having a bad dream and then I began to call out for Jesus.

Every time I said Jesus I could raise my head a little and then I came up off the bed and a dark shadow floated away from me. I hurried and flipped on the light.

It was almost like whatever that was, it tried to smother me. When the lighting came in, I saw the shadow clearly, it was a dark shadow and it moved fast.

I turned every light on in the house and went down stairs, turned the TV on, curled up on the couch and began praying and praying to the Lord to answer me about what just happened.

I am not able to explain what all took place, but I had a peace come over me and I fell into a deep sleep.

My views of life changed and I rose the next morning refreshed and a different light had entered my brain wave.

I was ready to start again.

Lord Jesus, I pray that each person who reads this will see You and have hope and want to start again...

Liz on the left and me having a birthday lunch for her unaware that this would be Liz's last birthday on earth.

Volume One

Is Fear in you?

Have you jumped at the sound of a door as the heat or air kicks on or off, and the door that you shut just opened? Have you been sitting in a silent room and something hit the window (you thought) or the room begins to crack and you look around as if you may not be the only one in the room or in your house?

Have you ever, while driving your vehicle, look over or even look down as though it seemed just for a moment, and you jerk the steering wheel to return back to the road? A blink, how quickly something can happen in a blink, a flash, in a time it took to look back. There is a song that I listen to on the Christian radio station that is titled, "It Happens in a Blink."

I look around and wonder what I was thinking as I grew into a young woman...

Where did life start? Where did my life begin? Or did it?

Volume One

I remember the three room home with a big (huge) fireplace which only seemed big to me, at the time, I am sure...to only watch my mother fill the fire to keep us warm since my dad was never home. Being a truck driver kept him away a lot. Not just a day or two, but days at a time could be a week at a time since I rarely can remember what he looked like just by pictures.

It is almost a mist, a shadow in which I could see so vaguely, but could not touch. The only thing I could really remember is him lying on the couch and telling my mother she needed to keep us kids quite since he had a bad headache.

I see pictures of him holding me as a small child, but remembering it, there is no recollection at all. I do remember my mom and dad had a couple who would come over and the big thing would be Krystal's in a bag. I remember playing outside on a swing and it being pitch dark outside. We lived out in the boonies. The cows would be the only thing you could hear, or our little dog, Peanut.

I do remember one incident with my brother when I thought my mother would almost kill my dad the day he kicked my brother for not handing him the correct tool. Can you imagine kicking your small son in the backend with a pointed boot? He could have injured him for life. I try to imagine what he was thinking, or was he?

Could my dad be that mean and unthoughtful? Who was he? Was he really our dad? Did he really want to be our dad? What can you make of such actions? Did my mother love him so much that she tried to not think of the way he really was? Maybe he was someone she dreamed up or was just living a make-believe life.

But, you never know what to do or say until you walk in someone else's shoes yourself. Shoes that none of us want to walk in, but do we? Can we? Or would we want to ... really?

There were a couple of times I remember when he was coming home, seemed as though maybe two times. My mother always would put that blue jar of 'Dippity Due' in her hair and rolled it up in those green and yellow rollers with bobby pins. I am sure some of you can remember this if you were born in the 50's and 60's. I can almost bet Lucille Ball, even Marilyn Monroe, or even Elizabeth Taylor wore them.

My mother's hair was a strawberry color and all the women wore their hair up in a 'bee hive' and wore those pointed Bat Woman glasses. My mother had a white pair and they were just as pointed as a pin. She always looked very pretty. She would put red lipstick on her most beautiful heart-shaped lips which made her very sexy all the way until she passed away.

Mother would wear those knee-knocker pants and bare feet. She hated shoes. She would get all of us a bath and put us to bed early so we never heard my dad come in or leave, at least I didn't. He must have come in late and left early in the mornings. He would be there just long enough to get her pregnant again.

It was like a feather in the wind. The time came and went.

You know, there are those who speak of a feather that they see when they say The Lord is there, or someone is there looking after them. But, when I speak of the feather, I speak of the feather floating in a mist, quickly floating around and around as though the wind takes it up and down never knowing where it may fall, if it ever falls.

Where is the feather that everyone speaks of, did I just miss it somehow?

Volume One

Remembering

I know that our house was so cold that when I was around 5 or 6 years old, when the fire would go out, instead of getting up to the cold, I would pee on the bed just to get warm for a few minutes and then would freeze, but I didn't want to put my feet on the cold floor. Our fire would go out in the night.

My mother would put us all in one bed. Can you imagine my mother and four children?

Since the bedroom was off the living room, the fire would go out and we would be without heat. My mom would tell us to stay in the bed until she got the fire started. Then we would all stand there with a blanket wrapped around us. I think of the year I flew to Haiti and all those little children not standing around a fire, but around the water trying to get cool from the heat.

How can this be? How can you leave four small children and not even worry if they ate, stayed warm or even had clean clothing. Days and days I cried out for all the children. There are so many children that are in different situations, and different environments that have no way of getting out.

They are trapped somehow, in bondage with drugs, alcohol, poor sleeping arrangements and being abused by who knows who.

As a child, we may remember one thing and not another. I enjoyed watching Lassie every afternoon after school my first year. I could not wait to go to school; I even got to ride the bus. Why are children so mean? Maybe they just like to pick. As soon as I would step up on the bus, they would sing "A Tisket, A Tasket, A Red and Yellow Basket." I never understood what that was all about.

I had to ride the bus my first year of school. I had to have crutches because I broke my ankle jumping in an empty swimming pool "Ouch!" Can you believe that back then we made up our own games? What a game! My mother carried me up a flight of stairs stating the whole time that I was a ton of lead. I was thin, tall and solid. Can you imagine carrying a seven year old at nine months pregnant?

Little memories in which I want to never forget, but yet somehow are forced way back in my mind so deeply that as I age they slowly seep to the surface. When they surface, I try to figure out what I did wrong or what did I do to cause the problem, or was the problem me? Maybe you can relate?

This is the story about my childhood, being a little girl, looking for someone, anyone who could replace my dad, I just wanted my dad. I know that I am not alone when you read about my growing up.

There are many more than just me who have experienced not having your mother or your father, or not having either of them. I thank The Lord every day that I had a mother and father, but, not having a mother and father.

Volume One

My Journey

That Made Me Who I Am Today

As I have told you, it began in a little three room home in Madison Tennessee off of Neely's Bend Road. I was seven years of age. We had a small black and white TV that I watched every day after school of my favorite show, Lassie.

There was a small room off the kitchen where my dad was going to put us a bathroom since we had no tub, no toilet, or wash area. We had to take the pot to the outhouse. I could hear my mom yell and say you better hurry up and not fall in, she would always try to scare us. She would say you never know what is in the bottom of that outhouse.

My brother and I were the oldest, so it was between the two of us, or my mom, to take out the pot. She would give us a bath in the kitchen sink. She would hook up the wringer washer machine to the kitchen sink and my brother would tell her when he grows up he is going to buy her a new washer.

When she would finish washing on a pretty day, we would go outside and want to play in the suds in the backyard. My mom said that it was a sink hole and it will take us under if we got too close, she told us to stay away and we did, being afraid that the sink hole would take us under. I wanted to play in the bubbles, how fun that would be!

I can still smell those sheets she hung and the feel of them when we would run back and forth through them when the wind would blow and the sheets would hit me in the face while I was running and my mother telling me the whole time she was going to tan my hide if I ran through those sheets one more time (guess we did again and again, it was too much fun).

She did let us get away with too much. It was almost like it went in one ear and out the other. We really needed a little more 'tan' on the hide you might say. She always tried to make it just right for us and I know she wished better things for us.

But I think she was happy just the way things were, even though we had nothing, we had everything. At least she thought we did, four children and a shack I would call it...nothing else mattered.

Volume One

My mother was in labor with me for 52 hours. She said they thought we were both dead and they insisted on a C-Section, but my mother refused. She would not let them. I am not sure what the rules of having a baby were back then but whatever they were, she got her way. I was born naturally and so were all my siblings, with me being the oldest, I was sissy, "The oldest."

This is where the enabling began to take care of others.

Volume One

Something Terrifying

Late one afternoon my mother had given us all a bath and told us we were going to my granny's to spend the night. My mom was all prettied up waiting for my dad. My sister was crying because she did not want to go, but my dad showed up and put us all in the car. My mom gave us all a kiss and told us she loved us.

And we were off.

But we kept driving and were not going in the direction to my granny's. I can remember him looking at me in the rearview mirror and I said, "Where are we going?" He said that plans had changed and he was taking us to a new big home and we were going to have a new mother.

I looked at him first with a "I don't think so look," then with tears I screamed, "**No!** *I want my mom and I want to go home.*" I kicked the seat and I screamed. As I was staring at him, he looked at me in the mirror and told me that I had better calm down and enjoy the ride.

It seemed for an eternity.

I looked at my brother in the front seat, and then I looked at my little brother in his car seat, and then my little sister, as a little girl of seven years old, I was wondering, "How am I going to take care of my little brother, my sister and my bubba? How could this be? I had never been to my first movie yet." All the emotions and feelings were swelling up inside of me until I fell into a deep sleep.

As I think about it today, I felt like an actor who was acting, but going through an acting scene and never even knowing what a movie was…

He made the comment that we were going to be happy: An adjective-delighted pleased, or glad: As over a particular thing to be happy to see a person. What person or persons was I supposed to be happy to see?

Strangers? Is this not what we try to teach our children to be careful and not talk to people that we do not know? All of this was overwhelming.

I tried to think about how my mother felt with my little brother being just a year old and me, the oldest at seven, had to be devastating. I could not imagine not knowing or seeing my boys for over two weeks (the amount of time we were gone).

Dad was pulling up at a huge tall building as I woke up. I sat straight up looking around. It was dark, but all I remember seeing was a sidewalk, I had no idea what that was, I thought the road was very close to the house.

He got us all out of the car and brought us into this lady's house that he called Martha and her five girls. It was so scary looking up at these tall people.

Then, one of the little girls, maybe a year or two older than me, came up to me and asked to see my 'Tommytale' which was my new doll I had just gotten for Christmas. The doll had a brush and tooth brush. I would pull her string and she would tell me to brush her hair or brush her teeth. She wore a watch that would say it was time for me to do this or that.

I was standing there thinking I had left my table and chairs and toaster and baby stroller. I just wanted to go home. Then all of a sudden this little girl grabbed my doll and said, "Come on let's go upstairs and play." She started taking my dress off

Volume One

...l, she said she wanted to change dresses with ...oll. By morning, my 'Tommy' had a new dress ...nd ink marks all over her arms.

I could not even tell you where we slept that night, or if I ever did. Sometimes I feel I may have had memory loss, just trying not to remember it all.

I know that I had come downstairs early that morning and heard my sister crying. I ran in the kitchen and I asked her what was wrong. She said, "Them girls was going to make her eat soggy cereal." I said, "No, you do not have to eat that." Then one of the girls told me, "Yes, she has to eat it." I said, "No, she does not and I told Tonya to get up." The girl said she was going to tell my dad and I looked at her and told her I did not care.

I was a bold little seven year old tot. I do know that I was very protective of my brothers and sister.

I felt like I was having a dream and could not wake up.

I changed my little brother, carried him around on my hip, being a little mom early it seemed. I remember at one point I had walked in a large bedroom where Martha and dad were lying in this bed with one of those radios above the headboard. My dad looked at me and said that he and Martha were getting married.

In the background that song was playing, the song in which I heard my mom say reminded her of my dad (Funny Face).

I stared at both of them hearing this song and I felt frozen like a Popsicle...

Starting to melt slowly, dripping one drop then another drop, and another and all I could think was I wanted my mother.

The days passed and still today I could not tell you what all went on. It is almost as though I put it totally out of my mind. I had even tried to sneak on a phone in the house to call my mom, but my dad's trucker buddy caught me.

There was so much going on around us all the time. Someone had even tried to break into one of the windows upstairs.

I guess I just zoned it all out.

I felt hopeless, lost, scared, and again, a lot of responsibility, it was a long two weeks.

Volume One

My Mother
The Frantic Search and Return

My mother had been out looking for us all that time. She had been to my grandmother's and they would not give her any information. She had been through so much trying to get us back.

She had a hysterectomy and had busted all her stitches open driving around looking for us.

No one would communicate with her. They had told her that they had no idea where we were. Yet my grandmother knew all along where we were. Being a mother-in-law, I could never keep such a thing, or even think my sons would do such a thing, and expect me to go along with it.

After all this stress, and finally getting us back, she ended up back in the hospital after coming home. She had developed "flee vitas" (Phlebitis).

She had to keep totally off her feet. I remember her wearing those ugly white stockings that you usually see older people wear. She had to keep her feet totally elevated and stay put as much as possible. We knew that she needed us to help her as much as we could.

My brother and I knew that, if nothing else, we needed to gather all that we could so that someone would stop and buy. That meant all of our toys. My mother had no money and there was no food in the house.

So we made a little booth at the end of our drive and put all our toys for sell.

We had one person pass by, Mr. Hunter, our local hometown grocery man, the owner of the only store close to our house. He knew my mother and father well.

Without hesitating, he bought everything we had and then brought us all kinds of goodies and also returned our toys.

What a man, I thought at seven years old, what a very generous man.

It felt like Santa Clause.

Volume One

How much did I know about Santa? Just that I had finally gotten the only doll that I ever wanted and then had to sell it. My first table and chairs, and a toaster...wow!

The biggest Christmas ever!

...and then had to let it go. You know we never even thought once about getting rid of our things, my brother nor I. It just never crossed our minds, just the fact that we had to take care of our mom and siblings.

But the act of God returned all our goods, including additional treats, because He does bless us in tri-folds.

There are so many children left in this world, whether it is by death of a parent, both parents, abandoned either from drugs or alcohol, maybe from mental problems or just walking away because they are not able to care for them.

There are so many different reasons that a child is left.

I told my father in a phone conversation one time, they are **LEFT OUT FOR THE WOLVES**.

Volume One

Wondering About it All

You know we can sit and wonder and try to figure it all out. Have you ever tried to figure someone out? Like a small child's likes and dislikes, whether they like black or white, beans or corn, rolls or cornbread, these are the small things.

Getting inside the core, deep in one's soul, almost like the commercial about the sinus guys who dance around fogging up our thoughts. Could this be what happens in those who just walk away and never look back?

As I get older, I do try to look at it all in perspective. Was my dad going through a crisis? How were he and my mother's relationship? Was it so bad that he had to avoid us like the plague?

He just totally stayed away.

Was he mentally disturbed? No one knows what was going on but him. Whether he will try to call one day or try to see us, I don't know. He calls my brother every now and then. But, I guess since he told me I was just like my mother, he may have a problem with giving me a call.

Does he ever think of what we are doing, or if we are okay? What about if we even have any feelings at all?

I guess I will always sit and wonder what my dad was thinking when he up and left four small children to fend for themselves, or to take us away and bring us back.

Just like picking out a puppy, you bring it home to see if it will work out and when you cannot take the responsibility for the puppy, it is too much, you return it or give it away.

Is this human?

Are there people out here who are so cold at heart that the only thing that matters is themselves? How can one do such a thing?

We could ask this question and ask this question, but I have a feeling we may not get the answer we are looking for.

As I have aged and raised my own children, I cannot even imagine. But, as I have said, we have to walk in that person's shoes and try to understand what was going on at the time of all the transitions.

Perhaps he and my mom had an unhealthy relationship, a breakdown, or was he self-centered?

How can anyone know when you cannot get any answers?

My mother died in 2007. That is when I called my dad and tried to talk to him and get some answers.

He beat around the bush about every question I tried to ask him. His response to me was that I sounded just like my mother. This went over and over in my head. I could hear his voice repeating and repeating those words about my mother.

What was he insinuating? I talked like my mother or spoke in a tone that was exactly like her?

He could not see me? He has no idea how I fix my hair or wear my makeup or what I like to wear. He has not a clue what I like or dislike.

Who is this man to tell me who I sound like or even act like?

I loved my mother dearly and she loved us, no doubt. But, the love that my mother provided, through her care for us and trying to love us, was the only way she knew how...

Volume One

What is Love?

We ask, "What is love?"

A word we throw around too often.

I love you, I love you, I love you. All I can do is look back and see a confused little girl who loved her mom dearly and needed her dad desperately, with all of this taking place in a little girl with a gigantic hole.

Being so young and fragile and you hear someone say to their children today, "Oh he or she is okay, they will get through it."

But, did they? Are they? Or maybe they are still battling with it like me in my mid-forties.

What a bummer for us to live in such turmoil. There are so many today who are still struggling with either the torture of their childhood, their teenage years, or even just dealing with life altogether.

Volume One

Then there are some who struggle right on up to their death. My mother struggled with depression, prescription drugs, and loneliness.

Although she had my step-dad, my mother was still alone inside. I do not think she ever got over my dad, even though she said she had. It was hard for her to trust.

We all may get to a point in life where we clam up inside, whether it is because of fear, jealousy or rebellion and we take it out on the ones who care for us the most.

My mother loved us dearly, I know this. But, she lived with an addiction to prescription drugs. You say, oh, this is a fluke, no one can be addicted to medication, or can they?

In life, we may have an addiction, whether it is food, drugs, money, sex, stuff, smoking, or bad language.

Anything can be an addiction if we let it.

Only we can let the control of whatever it could be take us over. It could be anything; even relationships can fall into this category, being addicted to another. We can be drawn into a world of, you name it.

It all goes together, somehow...**IF WE LET IT!**

After Dad Left

When my dad left, we had moved in an apartment house that had two apartments on the bottom and one on the top. We lived downstairs. There were two teenagers who lived upstairs that got to know us and hung out with us just about every night.

Mom had a job at a binding company. She was working and needed someone to keep all four of us. So, she got the little girl upstairs who was 14 to keep us. Her brother would come down and sit around while she was there.

Their parents were both alcoholics and would get drunk every night.

They would scream and yell at each other, and then they would call their children and scream at them. There was always glass breaking and shattering. There was even a gunshot one night. They were always into it.

I really felt sorry for them even at my young age.

My mother sort of took them under her coat. I remember her brother was 17. Cute I thought, but how could a child at my age know what cute was or would even have the feelings that I felt. All I know is that I would sit in his lap and stare at him and look at his dark hair and big eyes. How could an eight year old have such a desire to be wanted?

Just the fact that he would rub my hair, talk to me and laugh with me, this was the joy of my day.

My Aunt's daughter would stay with us and she had a son I would watch when she came over. She would tell me that I could have him if I would take care of him. And I did, I worked hard carrying him around. He was as big as I was.

I would feed him; change him, and play, we played so hard. I would pretend he was mine because she said I could have him.

I had some strange family.

As I think about it today, none of my family, on either side, wanted their children.

It seems that someone else always had their children. I am not sure what was going on in my little head, but the fact that I wanted to take care of that little boy.

I have always been a caregiver, always wanting to take care of something.

My mom would get so upset with me for bringing stray dogs or cats home. But she loved me, I know she did and she tried to take care of us.

But my mom could not deal with herself. She had been set up a couple of times with a few dates, but I know my mom loved my dad and she had a hard time with the dating scene.

Then my mom's sister fixed her up with my stepdad (he is still with us today). But, at 8 years old, this was a very hard time for me and my siblings.

I was a little demon. I can remember screaming, kicking, spitting, and becoming very loud. I wanted my daddy! I cried this every day, I would write him every day and tell him how much I loved him and wanted him home.

What was this tantrum that I had no control over? It was just as though I was possessed, taken over by some evil spirit.

Volume One

My Step-dad and Moving, Moving

My mother had to drag me from one point to another when I did not want to do what she wanted me to. I would throw a tantrum about everything. Nothing was good enough.

When mom and he married, he moved us into a town-house that was very nice.

We had upstairs and our own bedrooms. He bought new furniture and my mom even had a dishwasher and a washer and dryer. How can you beat that? But that was not good enough even for my mother.

We didn't stay there long at all. Then we moved again and again and again. I remember one place we moved and I had a fiend next door. She had a twin brother and she would wear a pretty white sweater and I wanted a white sweater so badly and look like her. She was so petite and spoke so softly.

Volume One

Her hair was short and curly and her brothers were so nice. Her mom and dad would check on her and tell her it was time to come in, it was getting dark.

I do not remember my mom calling me in and telling me it was too dark and for sure I had no dad to call.

They were such a close family.

We could do cartwheels and handstands just about every day. She had a poodle and I had a German Shepard. When she was called in, I would sit outside and play with him in the front yard. I would brush his teeth and comb him every day, but he got really big and aggressive. My mom said I had to chain him up, but he would get loose every time until the neighbors would call and complain.

One day when I got home from school (we had to walk to and from school), the law officers were at the house. I ran so hard and when I topped the hill of the driveway, they were bringing him toward the police car. I yelled and said, "What are you doing?" And the officer said that he was a K-9 and he would be a good police dog. He had to go with them.

I could not bear it. Something else was taken from me. Tiger would protect me.

It did reach the point when my mother would correct me; Tiger would growl at her and not let anyone very close to me at all. Of course, I loved it. He loved me, just like a human being. He was my best friend, just like my neighbor next door, just like two peas in a pod.

But again, another reason, who knows why, and we moved again.

I met another friend I wanted to be like. She was so pretty. We both did the blackboards after school and cleaned the classrooms. She was interested in the same boy I was. She shaved her legs and, of course, I begged mom to let me shave mine and I made sure he knew.

But his eyes were for the beautiful blonde, and she was. I wanted to be just like her.

I was never happy with me. I guess I thought if I was different maybe my dad would want me to be around.

I always wanted to be someone I was not.

Why would a child of my age, never really knowing what I really wanted, just know I wanted something different? It was not me, whoever 'me' was.

Volume One

What am I trying to say? How do I determine who the little girl is inside with the feelings that I felt, and the hurt that was going on?

Even to this day, I feel the same pain, especially when I see little girls without their dads.

I feel for these little ones. Maybe I am particular, but I can feel their pain. I want to protect all the little girls in the world, and I feel overwhelmed, helpless, thinking, "What can I do?"

There is nothing I can do but pray, and I have learned that through my every minute of life. The only peace and joy that I would get was through prayer.

The Lord has been my Father all these years and I know that there have been days that I did not listen to Him, just like a child would do his worldly father.

I have always been told that you never know what is going on in one's life. Do not ever wish you were anyone but the person God made, which is you?

There is only one you.

Volume One

We are all special in our own ways. There is a reason for all of us, and I know that He has a plan for me and He has one for you.

All of us are a beautiful creation.

After years had passed, I was working in Nashville on a night shift and I would stop in Shoney's on White Bridge Road and eat liver and onions. What a combination. I craved it for some reason.

I had eaten, paid, and went into the Ladies' Room and was in the stall next to the handicap stall. As I used the restroom, I thought about the lady struggling in the stall with her wheel chair.

I thanked God that was not me. As I came out of the stall, she was coming out and I helped her with the door.

When I looked at her, I thought, "Oh my Lord, it was her!" It was my friend, Beverly, the most beautiful girl who I wanted so badly to be. How could this be? In a wheel chair! She said she had been in a bad car accident.

I could have fallen to the ground! I wanted to grab her and hug her and tell her how I felt, and I did tell her she was an inspiration to me. She was in good humor and was doing a lot. She said she was just fine.

God shows us so much and sometimes we overlook it. We never give Him the thanks He so much deserves.

I think about how He shows me why things are not like I think they should be and why He brings those into our lives and gives us grace, not knowing at the time, at that moment, what is going on, but time brought it all together.

How He works is so awesome!

We need to stop and see what He has for us, not what everyone else is doing, or want to be how everyone else is. He made us all different and has a plan for us all, if we will just trust and believe in Him.

All the moves we made and all the different people we came in contact with have given me insight on how He is working in my life day to day. He showed me so much that day I ran into her.

The plans He had for her are not the plans He has for me, whether it be good or bad.

A lesson I have learned when I say I would like to be like this one or that one, I thank The Lord for who I am. I have not a clue what God wants in my life, but I am still and will wait for Him to show me what an awesome life He has chosen for me.

God is good all the time and I try to tell my children this today, whether they hear me or not, I will continue to 'preach' they call it, or speak religion, whatever that means...

I just know that until the day I breathe my last breath, I want my children to know that the only way is through The Lord Jesus. He has been my Father through all my bad decisions. I may have fallen, but He has always been there to pick me up.

Again, another move, and another move becomes like a natural thing to do. You make a friend and then it's time to move again. I am sure this is not news to some who live on the move throughout their lives. It is not a good feeling to be the new kid on the block, no matter where you go, you are always considered the new kid and there are things we 'new' kids have to deal with at every move.

There is a place where I wanted to run from, but felt stuck. We ended up in this place since my grandparents lived there, a place, to this day, I still do not enjoy. The only reason I go back is that my brother still lives there and I want to see my brother.

We had actually moved into a shack across from my grandmother's and again we did not have a toilet. I think my mother wanted to stay in the circle of her life with my dad, although we had everything.

It was a great Christmas that year and we all got bicycles. My step-dad worked hard and tried to make it good for us all. But, somehow my mom wanted to live in the past. We could never get away from the living situation. Finally they were building some low income houses in a very nice subdivision. My step-dad bought a little place in the subdivision. At the time, it was a nice little place and was a great neighborhood.

I did not have to change schools this time, I was so glad.

Even though I tried to make friends at school, I always seemed out of place somehow. I tried to make friends with the girls and they seemed to shun me. I always seemed to have boys for friends. I never understood why they never let me in their little groups.

Have you ever felt that you were in a place where you were very different? That you never fit in somehow.

Volume One

For some reason, I always seemed alone. I stayed outside from daylight to dark, unless I went to school. I would get on the bus and my mom would be sitting in this old checkered green chair drinking her coffee and smoking a cigarette, and when I got off the bus she would still be in that chair with a cigarette and by that time, a glass of tea.

Signs of Addiction

As I said, I know my mom loved me but she was dealing with a lot going on inside her. My mom always complained about having pain somewhere. Almost on a daily basis, and when her mom died, it seemed as though she really went down, she changed so much. She ended up going to numerous doctors where she received several different medications.

My mom did try to keep it together and she did cook (she was a really good cook). She loved to cook. But, at one point it got to where we did not have food in the house. I remember putting catchup on a cracker because there was no food in the house.

The more I think about those days, I feel it was just the beginning, my mother had spent all the money on meds. Can I prove this? No. But I am sure that my step-dad would tell you this is true.

My mother could afford cigarettes and what she wanted. I would find candy bars hidden in the cabinet stashed way back.

I guess that is why I crave sweets so much today. I would sneak a bar of candy and go to the bathroom and lock the door and eat it and wrap the paper up in toilet paper and put it deep in the trash.

Can you imagine the little children today who have nothing to eat and they sneak in the garbage or trash to find something to eat? I know I was never that hungry, at least I think we always came up with something to throw together. My addiction may have started early.

I guess addiction could be anything.

I can understand an alcoholic wanting and thinking about the next drink, or a drug addict for the next fix. When I think about sugar, as in a cookie, candy bar, or piece of pie, and will go all the way to the store to get it, that is bad.

No one knows what one is battling or thinking or going through. We never know why one acts, says, or even responds in the way that they do.

Never judge a book by its cover. It is the pages that you go through and read that brings out the true story.

We all have a story.

Volume One

I know at an early age, I did some crazy things. Why would a child sneak and smoke or drink when they think no one will find out? As a child, I never really liked the cigarette thing, but because everyone did it, you always want to see what it's like.

For some reason I was an adventurous little girl. I always wanted attention from the opposite sex. It was right after I started my menstrual cycle, my mom would let me go to the neighbor's house that was 18 or 19 and was married to a drummer in a band and he was always gone. So I would sit with her on a Friday or Saturday night while he was gone and she would get out his Playgirl books and show me all kinds of things and tell me that it does not hurt and feels good.

The Barn

A year had passed and I had been given a note from one of my best friends in school who was a male. He had given me a love note and said that he had liked me for a long time and wanted me to be his girlfriend. I accepted and was so excited that I was really wanted and someone really liked me.

But we all know life can be a fantasy.

He was also my friend. (The boys would always tell me about their girl problems. I should have become a counselor. Up to this day I have more individuals that confide in telling me all this stuff and I have not a clue, but I guess I have always been a good listener.) A girl had broken up with him and he was sad, but not sad enough I guess.

My bubble busted the night I went to my first party. I had begged my mother to let me go. I was scared and excited all at the same time.

Volume One

It was Halloween weekend and we were invited at some friend's house. Halfway through the party, everyone was walking to the barn behind the house.

How everything can happen in a blink.

We went into the barn and lay in a bed of hay. He started kissing me which was nice. But then he started really kissing me hard and then touched me. Without a second thought, I had hit him across the face and jumped up and wanted to go home.

I remember going toward the burning fire by myself and I was cold and alone, crying and never wanting to see him again. Again, at 12 I felt that I did not fit in anywhere. Was it because I felt invaded? Did I feel that this was wrong, or was I a baby? I did not even want him as a friend again. What was that?

Why had this been an on-going trip for me? In all my 12 years, I had searched and searched over and over, just like all little girls my age when there is no father in their lives.

All around us there are girls who search for love in all the wrong places. They search their entire lives and never find the real true love until they find The Lord.

Babysitting

I started keeping a little boy across the street. The mother had asked if I would be interested in making a little spending money. Mom said she thought I was still a little young, but since they would be there and I was right across the street, it should be okay.

I had kept him twice, and then one weekend I had to put him to bed early and they had me a roll-out couch in the living area.

She had called me into their bedroom and asked me if I would want to watch TV with them. So I lay at the end of the bed and they put in a flick movie and the dad of the little boy started to rub my legs and up close to my panties. I laid there frozen, I felt numb. I tried to move slowly toward the edge of the bed.

I told them I was tired and was going to bed. He said, "You sure you do not want to play?" I said, "No I am tired." I never kept the little boy again. I avoided them like the plague and never told anyone.

I guess I thought I had talked my mom into taking care of this little boy so it was my fault. I caused this by being over at a stranger's house and keeping their baby. It seemed when things would happen out of the ordinary, I would blame myself for some reason, and like it was my fault that these grown adults were taking advantage of a 12 year old.

This is why I feel when I run into girls who are that age, I try to, in a roundabout way, let them know they are beautiful and wait on The Lord to bring them their soul mate. Throughout the years this has happened to so many young girls and no one ever knew.

I see it today on the news and cringe with fear for them. Why can they not tell? Why did I not tell? Why do we feel so secretive about the whole situation? Is it fear, blame, or shame?

Why is it that we cannot confess this immorality that has happened to us?

I look back and compare today with my life then and we somehow feel that our fathers or mothers did not give us this attention and when someone else does, we are not sure how to handle it. But somehow it feels good and bad at the same time. Somehow knowing this is wrong and should be told but, keep it inside like a great big secret that somehow follows us around like a shadow on our back no matter where we go. Eventually we start another day and go on to the next thing in which we have not a clue.

Let's try it again; this time a single lady asked me, she is safe for sure.

So I started keeping another little boy, but the mother was single and lived by herself, so I felt no fear. She would go out and I would stay and play mommy. When she would leave I would feed him and give him a bath and play until he would finally want me to rock him and he would go to sleep.

Then I would put on her sexy lingerie and pretend I was the mom and I would dress just like the women in those magazines that I had been shown.

Until one night, I was playing dress up when someone knocked on the door. I asked who it was and he said that he was a friend of the lady I was keeping her baby.

Back then I never thought a thing about it.

I had a house coat over me and was covered. I opened the door and there was a tall handsome guy, being very friendly and asking me if I was alone. Naïve as I was, I said, "Just me and the baby and he is asleep." My friend was out and would be back soon.

He said you are very pretty, what do you have on under that robe? I slowly stepped back when he rubbed my face and pulled my long hair back away from my face. His eyes were so convincing of anything, but how would I know such a thing.

I had the music on with Rod Stewart playing. He was so gentle, but again, how did I know what that meant either? He kissed me and I let him.

He was old enough to be my daddy. He slowly picked me up and carried me into the bedroom where he laid me down and he kissed me and rubbed me from head to toe. Why did I not run or slap him? Why did I not say, "No?" I let him rub and lick me from head to toe just like the women and men did in those magazines. I felt so loved and so protected by a big handsome man.

I did not know he was a married man and lived two doors down from my house, but I was saved by grace. There was a knock at the front door. It was another guy friend of mine. How did he know that I was there? The man left and this friend came in and tried to do the same thing. I made him leave.

What was I thinking? There had been two men trying to take advantage of me in one night and I was only 13 by this time, almost 14.

When I read what I just put on this page, it brought a thought to my mind. What was this little girl thinking in her mind? What do a lot of little girls think who want to have their dads so badly that any attention from any man... any man?

There is a pain within which no one knows unless they have experienced it. Not knowing what a dad was supposed to do or say, I took all or anything I could get, a kiss, a touch, in any shape or form.

Was I calling to my dad as I did when he left? I would call out to him and nothing, nothing at all. "I want my daddy." All I wanted was for him to love me and give me the attention that a dad is supposed to give their child.

Was I a disturbed child?

Maybe.

Was I so caught up in the loss of my father that my whole childhood became a blur? Everything around me was almost like a Fairytale, Cinderella being my favorite movie.

Where are the Dads?

I know the first movie my mom took us to see was E. T. I wanted to call out and say phone home. I wanted to go home to the only place I barely remembered. Is this how The Lord made us, wanting to be wanted, loved, touched, a soft word of encouragement, safety, protection from our dads, our moms, being a close family?

All of this is but a vapor, all but a Fairytale in most little girls' homes. Put out to the wolves for whomever to devour, destroy, and be treated in any way. What other way do we know? How were we taught a father should be or act to us, we weren't, I wasn't, a lot of others too.

I think of some of the ways of trying to get love and how I went about it for so many years. I ask, "Why am I still here and why did I hurt so many?" Oh the pain.

Hurt, deserted, abandonment, neglect, a hole that is so deep that even mounds of dirt will not be able to fill the depth, the thing about the sore is that its scab falls off, but then it comes back, never healing until we bring The Lord into our life.

I had to call out to The Father above because here I had no earthly Father, a biological father like you see in 'Leave it to Beaver' or 'Bewitched,' 'Mary Tylor Moore,' and 'Andy Griffin.'

Where are those dads?

Writing my dad every day and not hearing from him became so emotional. You can say just get over it, but do we?

I have worked hard on covering my memories, what I remember. I feel I put up a mental block where I would live in a fantasy world in which I could pretend. And I did a lot of pretending even to the point of telling little fibs. Make believe stories because I never wanted anyone to know who I really was. It seemed as though there were too many perfectionists in the world for me.

I can close my eyes and see the little house on Neeley's Bend. As I got older, I remember I was in my twenties, I went back to see only a field. As I was sitting there thinking about what could have been and if I would have been different. If I could have known The Lord sooner and could I have been protected from all the evil that I have encountered as I traveled alone without my dad.

A man had pulled up as I stepped out of my car and he asked me if I was the little girl who used to live here and I looked at him, not knowing who he was, and still to this day I have not a clue. I did not even get out of my mouth, "Who are you?" He said, "I recognized you." And then he left.

As I put my words on paper, I ask myself, "Who was that man" Why did I not ask him who he was? So much we put deep inside, that we find it hard to reveal.

I know The Lord puts those in our lives for reasons, maybe even for a season. But however He intends to get our attention, He knows the ropes. One of the reasons we miss out and sometimes miss the open door is we seem to fill our lives with so much "to do" stuff and not focus on the job that our Lord has for us to do.

We have to be still and listen. He is speaking to us whether it is through someone else or just a small still voice, or maybe in a dream.

We just need to be focused and pay attention to everything around us. Think about the ones who are in need and the ones who may need us in other ways.

We all need each other, no matter what.

To this day I ask The Lord, "Can you hold me together? Can Your hands reach down this far and save me from this world?"

I have been speaking of our last move, before it all began, after all my adventures with the babysitting from this move, I spoke of us going to the High School, riding the school bus and being picked on, and had gum thrown in my hair.

Volume One

7th Grade

I hated going to school.

School had started back and it was time to get back into the school. I had failed 7th grade and had tried out for cheerleader the next year. My cousin and I both made the team, but our teacher told us that we had better make the grades or she was going to give us a hard time.

She would keep my cousin sitting on her desk for hours. She never told me if she bothered her.

We had a choice if we wanted to go to the High School and we did. We went on and were with the High School crew. I still had to ride the School Bus every day and every day I got bubble gum thrown in my hair by the bigger kids on the back of the bus. The older crew...

One afternoon, I was close to the back of the bus and one of the girls yelled and said, "Hey virgin girl" and threw gum in my hair. How can people be so cruel? But kids are very cruel to one another.

That is when my life began to change. They had thrown gum in my hair and I never looked back. I was just sitting on the edge of my seat and I watched each one get on the bus. Then a guy looked at me and said, "Scoot over," and I did, he looked back and told the kids in the back to leave me alone...

I thought he was a hero, he protected me...and he wanted me to meet him on the hill at the old house in the field...and ...

I debated for a long time. I was in the front yard looking for four-leaf clovers.

I wanted that attention so badly. When I got there, it happened so fast, I cannot even remember what happened, or even tell you if I felt a thing. I just remember the blood and him saying, "I have to go."

And he left me there, nothing to wipe with, just standing there.

What just happened? What is wrong with me? Why do I just keep getting left?

Volume One

You know when you are watching a movie and the camera circles around the person and they are just standing there in a daze, or just shock of what just happened? I was a little girl, 14 years of age, in the middle of the woods, in an abandoned house with the windows broken out, and no doors. You could see the bottom of the ground through the wood floors.

What was I thinking at this very moment? What was going on inside? Hurt, deserted, anger, loved? What just happened? This is what happens to so many young girls.

Was this rape? No, I met him. Was I forced? No, I let him do this to me. Why would a young girl of my age go along with this?

I ran home as quickly as I could, not looking back. I was just thinking and running, thinking and running. I was just thinking and running, thinking and running.

About what? Would I ever see him again? Is this the beginning of what?

Although I met him again and again and just felt for a moment that I had someone who wanted to see me and talk to me, touch me, and felt that I was the only one, but he was young and I was young and I had become pregnant, and he was gone...

Is this what I have learned about love? Abandonment, this is life, nothing lasts forever, nothing is true, nothing is solid, not even my own father.

His mother said it wasn't her son's baby... that it could have been anyone's...

I understand that now that I am older. I may have thought the same thing his mother did; Mothers are always protective of their children.

The attention, the need that we so much strive for and need from our dads and our mothers, we seek in others and other places...

Not only do young girls seek the attention from others, such as men, and in these days, not only male and female attraction, but drugs and alcohol.

Almost 99% of the ones I knew in school who did not have their mother or father giving them directions and supporting them (letting them roam the neighborhoods and getting into things that were not good for them) ended up in jail from drugs or alcohol. Or, they have ended up in both as I did and am living proof that living without my dad had a very big impact on my behavior.

I was a very rebellious and hateful smart tale, as I may say and I put that lightly. I was like a little demon from hell. I hit, screamed, bit, and lashed out at my mother and step-dad. My repeated words were, "I want my dad," someone who never gave me the time of day and still does not until this day.

In going back through my thoughts on what has happened to me, I remember babysitting... and the knock at the door, I was only 13. Why did I lay there and let him take control? How far would he have gone if we were not interrupted? Was I that gullible that I just wanted the feeling of someone being close and hugging me and giving me the attention that I had so longed for?

That was not the only time, different ones approached me with affection. I took it anyway I could, I took it. Why was such a little girl with no morals lost in the midst of the world?

I see little girls today at 13 and I want to protect them so badly.

How many of us were out there and had no direction? How many little girls did not get away from the older man, or the over active teenage boy? What do little girls face today that have no father in their home, the neglect and the loneliness that one feels as I did?

I only knew my dad from pictures and barely remember him when I was a child. I wanted my dad. I would cry for him and wish he would just call or come and get me. I pretended a lot and felt like an outcast.

I went from a young 13 fragile little girl into a woman with a small child, off to work, trying to take night classes to learn and educate myself, and feeling as though I struggled with my every step.

I questioned why everything I did or would become involved in, seemed as if I could barely pass or get by. It seemed I was always struggling trying to be a part of this world.

But no matter how hard I tried, I always felt out of place.

How many children start to school with a broken foot from jumping off a hay wagon into an empty pool, busted my chin jumping off my mother's flour bend trying to be Superman? Good grief, I was a little girl. What was I doing always trying to prove myself?

I could go on and on with the illusions that one little girl can and could have. I think of my little granddaughter as I write this book and how I know I cannot protect her of all the things of this world, but my prayers are all I have to give her and to tell her of the love of Jesus.

Volume One

Pregnant

I found out I was pregnant. But, he denied it and his parents said it could be anyone's. I had never been with anyone.

What have I done?

This is what the world begins to think of you. A little hot girl who can't keep her legs closed. An outsider is what I felt, and back then you could not go to school pregnant. You had to be home schooled, and I was. I was apart from all my school mates.

I was different now. I had no true friends.

Who would want to hang around a pregnant girl?

I told my mother on my 15th birthday.

They had taken me to Long John Silvers, since it was my favorite. But I was about to faint standing at the counter. I had told the lady taking my order that I had to go the bathroom for a minute. I stood in the bathroom feeling like I could throw up at any time. I went back out and told the lady that I did not feel good and would send my dad in to get my meal.

I ran to the car and my mom said, "Where is your food?" I said you are going to have to go in and get it, I could not wait. I felt as though I was going to hit the floor. I laid in the backseat of the car.

I can see her now; she turned around in the front seat and said my name, "Are you pregnant?" I looked at her and said, Mom, I didn't know, still thinking in the back of my head, "Oh my Lord, what have I done?"

I called my friend who lived across from our house (she was 18). I told her something was wrong and what I had done.

She asked me if I thought I could be pregnant. I did not know. She said she would pick me up a pregnancy test and for me to come over that evening and spend the night and we would check it the next morning.

Of course it showed positive. I cried, but yet I felt like I now had someone to love and who would love me back.

The next day my mom and I talked back and forth all day. Trying to break the news was very hard. I started to cry like a baby, I felt so bad. She said that I needed to go to the doctor and get checked. So she made me an appointment and it was positive.

It was almost as though I had been given the world. Almost as though I had something that no one could ever take from me. I was happy and did not even have a clue where or what this event of happiness was. I just knew I felt really good. Yet I was scared and unsure of what was going to happen.

I knew my grandmother and aunts had been calling my mother and telling her that she needed to do something about this. I was too young and my life was ruined.

Then, my aunt, my grandmother and my mother all met late one afternoon. They all sat down and one at a time started telling me what my life was going to be like and how I needed to finish school and get an education.

They said that a child would hinder me and my life would be over. My whole life would change and I would live a miserable life.

They started telling me all about their lives and how bad it was, and if they would have known what they knew that day, they would have done things differently, and then everything would be so much better.

These are grown women who all had lived an unhappy life.

What makes one live in such an environment? Is it money? Is it loneliness? Was it the thought of being alone, or just a thing to do?

I know I watched my mother live a lonely life. She loved us all and I know she loved my step-dad, but there was something still missing. I know when we talked about my dad you could see the anger rise in her eyes. My mother loved my dad. But she needed someone to help with four small children. She even told my step-dad that she did not love him but needed someone to help with us.

She always said that she grew to love my step-dad. But what kind of love was it? I would see her happy sometimes and then some days not very happy. She would sit a lot and stay inside. I know she thought about my dad and what would have been or could have been.

I feel like my mom wasted her life and I think about how so many people live day to day and wonder what may have been, could have been, or should have been. Who knows how our lives would be if we would just give it to The Lord? Instead, we try to put it together ourselves.

I know that there are so many who live in this situation every day, whether it is because of the children or just because they have no other choice because the one they love does not love them back.

After everyone had coaxed my mother and me into going to the abortion clinic, and having all the tests and reviewing the literature...

What if on that day, I would have not been too far along and they would have taken my son? How would my life be? I would think about him and wonder what would have been.

Instead: That day, lying on that table, after going through the drawing of blood and watching the movie on the procedure, I was scared and all I could do was lay there and ask The Lord not to let it happen.

The doctor came in and never even touched me. He said that I was too far along and that the procedure could not be done. I jumped up and put my clothes on and could only think about taking care of my baby. Oh my Lord, I am still a baby, taking care of a baby…

How did I know who to ask? I never heard my family talk about The Lord. Church was not part of our lives. I remember going to a Vacation Bible School one year and maybe a few times to a church that spoke of the way we were dressed.

I never really was interested in attending a church.

But somehow on that day, The Lord was in that room with His presence all around me and covering my son, the son who has grown to be a very bright, wonderful young man.

Volume One

Something Missing, Something Found

Still, after all of this, I never thought about The Lord again until I knew I was missing something in which I have missed all my life, a Father, and He became that to me and still is to this day.

I had to lean on His understanding and not my own.

For some reason I have always thought I was different. I would sit in front of the TV just as close as I could get and would think I was saying every word that they were saying. It is almost like I could look at someone and I could feel what they were thinking or even could feel the evil or the good in someone.

Do not get me wrong, I know I am not some sort of special person, but in some ways I think I am, since The Lord has covered me and protected me throughout my life. I know some people may think one is crazy and maybe we all are at a point, in a good way that is.

I went for years wondering what was wrong with me and I went through several marriages and several jobs. I was looking for something that I could not find.

I cried out for my dad a lot of those times when I was alone and felt that I could not go on. It happened one fall when my youngest son was around four. I had just taken all that I could and I could not stand it anymore. I had gone to the doctor and told her I was scared and was scratching my arms until they would bleed.

I felt as though I was way out of control and could not function to the point I was not sure I could even take care of my own children any longer. She immediately put me in the hospital and said that I was about to have a nervous breakdown.

I had finally drawn the line; I had let too many people try to control my life.

I had gotten out of the hospital and was going to try to start at the beginning. But, what is the beginning? Where do you start when your whole world has fallen apart?

I had been to church and was active in The Word and my husband, at that time, was trying, but I was not happy with any part of this life.

I did not love this man I called my husband.

I mean, I cared, that was always my problem. I tried to help (men) people and one of my ways of trying to take care of them was sex. It always seemed that was how I communicated with any male subject.

I tried to be there physically instead of mentally.

What was that? You know I have heard of several actresses who had married several times and had different relationships and you hear people talking about the situation, "How can they do such a thing?"

Never say it could not happen to you because it can happen to anyone.

So many women are stuck in a body that they have no control wishing that somehow or someway things could be different.

I say this because I always thought I was the only one, different from all other women. But as the years go by, there are so many women just like me. Some commit suicide and end up taking depression medicine because they have become so out of control.

They believe what other people say.

They have been told that they are beautiful and then, in the same words, told that they are unworthy, fat, skinny, they are condemned that they are not smart, need this or that. They are told that nothing about them is of any value. There are men that down their women and there are women who can be so cruel,

... Not knowing that they are pulling that person into a hole...

Then they draw themselves into their own world of isolation, work, alcoholism, or even to the point of just being in relationships just to have a mate.

This is true. It happened to me so many times.

I was married five times and in all of them for some sort of reason other than real love.

I just wanted to have someone to love, but never had them love me back.

Volume One

Have you ever been married just to call someone your husband?

I always wanted to have a good husband to care for me, but it seemed I got into relationships where I had to take care of them, whether it was financial, physical, or even mental. I was always there to take care of a situation.

That attention, that touch, that 'not being lonely syndrome,' I guess you could say.

After my son, Rocky was born; I took night classes and ended up getting my GED.

I would teach myself how to work a job. I had some good jobs and was too young to realize what I had.

I made it through the relationships and was sort of staying away from the dating scene. Rocky was 8 and I felt that I needed to just focus on him.

Then it happened.

It was New Year's Eve and I did not even go out. I had stayed home and my sister, who lived with me, brought some friends home with her.

The Beginning of my Nightmare

I am not saying that in a bad way, I fell in love with a boy who was 5 years younger than I, and ended up getting married and becoming pregnant on my wedding night.

I became so consumed that everything around me was as though I was slowly losing minute by minute.

I worked the night shift and had a great job, but I was accused of everything under the sun and I was going to work. Every night was the same old stuff. I had become swollen and ended up taking a volunteer layoff.

I was out of work until Darren was 6 months old. Then I was coached into going to work. Every day I was told I needed to find a job. I had always worked and I put in for a job and made really good.

But again, my marriage was an accusing and mentally abusive relationship every day.

Volume One

I met a gentleman at work and had no intentions of doing what I did. But somehow I was coaxed into the sin... adultery...

I had already made the decision that I was going to give my husband a divorce and wished I would have waited, but I did not. He had moved out but drove by one night and saw this man leaving our home. He came in and took what I felt I deserved.

My own husband raped me and hit me and I lay there and took it.

I had done wrong and felt that whatever he did, I needed to be punished. We had gone to his parents the next day and I even tried to explain what I had done and my husband stood up and just hit me several times.

All his mom would say was, "Don't do that." And his dad just sat there.

Somehow I felt as though I was trapped. My son was just 2 and I had made a big mistake. I could not even be faithful in one thing... my marriage.

I had gone to work the next morning with my face black and blue and my eyes were swollen and sore from all that had happened. Still, no one ever cared about the fact that I was hurt.

They looked at me as if I was an alien.

I had no one who wanted to protect me or love me. I just had to hold my head up and do my job the best I could without distractions.

I tried to be better and be the best wife I could, but no matter what I did, it was not good enough. This just gave him another excuse to drink.

Drinking was so much more important to him than his family. I had tried all that I could.

I even started thinking of ways I could kill him and not go to prison and leave my sons.

Then one night my oldest son said he had enough of seeing me treated the way I was treated and he got a bat and headed toward my husband. I caught him and I said…

This is it. Things have to be different. I started looking for me a home. I had a friend who knew someone that was trying to sell their home. I was determined that I was getting away from what was hurting me. I told him the day I was moving, if you love me and want to be a family, you will come with me and stop drinking.

But, he stood at the door and watched me leave with his beer and cigarette in his hand and did not even try to stop us or tell us he loved us.

I pulled out and left it all. I started over. I just wanted my children to enjoy their childhood.

Childhood? What did I even know about childhood? Did I ever live a normal childhood or is there such a thing?

Could 'Leave it to Beaver' be a classic image of a perfect family? Or Lassie, the loving dog that protected her owner at all risk? Or The Andy Griffith show where Opie seemed to be very happy and did not have a mother?

I am not sure if a mom or dad is the real answer since there are so many children who are being raised by the grandparents or other relatives within the family.

What else do we linger for? Love, someone to tell us that we mean something to them, that their child means something to them, this was not the case.

I could never get that so-called love that I was searching for, the desires of my heart, you would say, trying to change someone is impossible.

No matter what you do, you cannot change a person into who you think they should be or do.

Prayer is all I could do and my prayers did not help.

Why did my prayers not help? I did not have the relationship with God that I needed to pray for my husband.

I had no idea what it meant to communicate with The Lord. I questioned why my prayers were not answered and had no idea that I was not praying correctly.

Praying correctly?

This is true; I prayed prayers that were not answered because I could not communicate with God. He was not hearing me. I was still carrying sin in my life.

I had not repented for my sins and had not asked for forgiveness. I had not prayed for myself to be changed.

I had to deal with me…

Volume One

And I am still dealing with me today.

Tessa Marie Grisham

Born
May 19, 1964

Volume One

Rocky and Darren...

Gifts from God

"Go home to your family
and tell them how much the Lord has done for you,
and how he has had mercy on you"
Mark 5:19 (NIV)

Volume One

Tessa - 4
Harold Lee, Jr. - 3
Tonya - 1-1/2

Tessa Marie Grisham
Harold Lee, Jr. Grisham

Tessa Marie Grisham
18

Tessa Marie Grisham Pregnant with her firstborn (Rocky)

Tessa Marie Grisham Pregnant with her second son (Darren)

Volume One

Rocky
1-1/2
Tessa's
Firstborn

Darren
1-1/2
Tessa's
Second
Son

Volume One

Scriptures for Father's

Bible verses about being a godly dad and husband. These passages of Scripture declare what God intended for men and how we can celebrate our fathers.

Joshua 1:9 (KJV)
9 Have not I commanded thee? Be strong and of a good courage; be not afraid, neither be thou dismayed: for the Lord thy God is with thee whithersoever thou goest.

Psalm 103:13 (KJV)
13 Like as a father pitieth his children, so the Lord pitieth them that fear him.

Deuteronomy 6:6-9 (KJV)
6 And these words, which I command thee this day, shall be in thine heart:
7 And thou shalt teach them diligently unto thy children, and shalt talk of them when thou sittest in thine house, and when thou walkest by the way, and when thou liest down, and when thou risest up.
8 And thou shalt bind them for a sign upon thine hand, and they shall be as frontlets between thine eyes.
9 And thou shalt write them upon the posts of thy house, and on thy gates.

Joshua 24:15 (KJV)

[15] And if it seem evil unto you to serve the Lord, choose you this day whom ye will serve; whether the gods which your fathers served that were on the other side of the flood, or the gods of the Amorites, in whose land ye dwell: but as for me and my house, we will serve the Lord.

Deuteronomy 1:29-31 (KJV)
[29] Then I said unto you, Dread not, neither be afraid of them.
[30] The Lord your God which goeth before you, he shall fight for you, according to all that he did for you in Egypt before your eyes;
[31] And in the wilderness, where thou hast seen how that the Lord thy God bare thee, as a man doth bear his son, in all the way that ye went, until ye came into this place.

Proverbs 3:11-12 (KJV)
[11] My son, despise not the chastening of the Lord; neither be weary of his correction:
[12] For whom the Lord loveth he correcteth; even as a father the son in whom he delighteth.

Proverbs 14:26 (KJV)
[26] In the fear of the Lord is strong confidence: and his children shall have a place of refuge.

Psalm 127:3-5 (KJV)
[3] Lo, children are an heritage of the Lord: and the fruit of the womb is his reward.

⁴ As arrows are in the hand of a mighty man; so are children of the youth.
⁵ Happy is the man that hath his quiver full of them: they shall not be ashamed, but they shall speak with the enemies in the gate.

Proverbs 22:6 (KJV)
⁶ Train up a child in the way he should go: and when he is old, he will not depart from it.

Exodus 34:6-7 (KJV)
⁶ And the Lord passed by before him, and proclaimed, The Lord, The Lord God, merciful and gracious, longsuffering, and abundant in goodness and truth,
⁷ Keeping mercy for thousands, forgiving iniquity and transgression and sin, and that will by no means clear the guilty; visiting the iniquity of the fathers upon the children, and upon the children's children, unto the third and to the fourth generation.

Ephesians 5:25-33 (KJV)
²⁵ Husbands, love your wives, even as Christ also loved the church, and gave himself for it;
²⁶ That he might sanctify and cleanse it with the washing of water by the word,
²⁷ That he might present it to himself a glorious church, not having spot, or wrinkle, or any such thing; but that it should be holy and without blemish.

28 So ought men to love their wives as their own bodies. He that loveth his wife loveth himself.
29 For no man ever yet hated his own flesh; but nourisheth and cherisheth it, even as the Lord the church:
30 For we are members of his body, of his flesh, and of his bones.
31 For this cause shall a man leave his father and mother, and shall be joined unto his wife, and they two shall be one flesh.
32 This is a great mystery: but I speak concerning Christ and the church.
33 Nevertheless let every one of you in particular so love his wife even as himself; and the wife see that she reverence her husband.

Ephesians 6:1-4 (KJV)
6 Children, obey your parents in the Lord: for this is right.
2 Honour thy father and mother; which is the first commandment with promise;
3 That it may be well with thee, and thou mayest live long on the earth.
4 And, ye fathers, provoke not your children to wrath: but bring them up in the nurture and admonition of the Lord.

Genesis 2:24 (KJV)
24 Therefore shall a man leave his father and his mother, and shall cleave unto his wife: and they shall be one flesh.

Volume One

1 Corinthians 13:1-13 (KJV)

13 Though I speak with the tongues of men and of angels, and have not charity, I am become as sounding brass, or a tinkling cymbal.

2 And though I have the gift of prophecy, and understand all mysteries, and all knowledge; and though I have all faith, so that I could remove mountains, and have not charity, I am nothing.

3 And though I bestow all my goods to feed the poor, and though I give my body to be burned, and have not charity, it profiteth me nothing.

4 Charity suffereth long, and is kind; charity envieth not; charity vaunteth not itself, is not puffed up,

5 Doth not behave itself unseemly, seeketh not her own, is not easily provoked, thinketh no evil;

6 Rejoiceth not in iniquity, but rejoiceth in the truth;

7 Beareth all things, believeth all things, hopeth all things, endureth all things.

8 Charity never faileth: but whether there be prophecies, they shall fail; whether there be tongues, they shall cease; whether there be knowledge, it shall vanish away.

9 For we know in part, and we prophesy in part.

10 But when that which is perfect is come, then that which is in part shall be done away.

11 When I was a child, I spake as a child, I understood as a child, I thought as a child: but when I became a man, I put away childish things.

¹² For now we see through a glass, darkly; but then face to face: now I know in part; but then shall I know even as also I am known.
¹³ And now abideth faith, hope, charity, these three; but the greatest of these is charity.

Exodus 14:13 (KJV)
¹³ And Moses said unto the people, Fear ye not, stand still, and see the salvation of theLord, which he will shew to you to day: for the Egyptians whom ye have seen to day, ye shall see them again no more for ever.

1 Corinthians 16:13 (KJV)
¹³ Watch ye, stand fast in the faith, quit you like men, be strong.

Ephesians 6:11-18 (KJV)
¹¹ Put on the whole armour of God, that ye may be able to stand against the wiles of the devil.
¹² For we wrestle not against flesh and blood, but against principalities, against powers, against the rulers of the darkness of this world, against spiritual wickedness in high places.
¹³ Wherefore take unto you the whole armour of God, that ye may be able to withstand in the evil day, and having done all, to stand.
¹⁴ Stand therefore, having your loins girt about with truth, and having on the breastplate of righteousness;
¹⁵ And your feet shod with the preparation of the gospel of peace;

[16] Above all, taking the shield of faith, wherewith ye shall be able to quench all the fiery darts of the wicked.

[17] And take the helmet of salvation, and the sword of the Spirit, which is the word of God:

[18] Praying always with all prayer and supplication in the Spirit, and watching thereunto with all perseverance and supplication for all saints;

Has anyone ever told you that God loves you and that He has a wonderful plan for your life? If you were to die this very second, do you know for sure, beyond a shadow of a doubt, that you would go to Heaven?

The Holy Bible reads "for all have sinned and come short of the glory of God" and "for the wages of sin is death, but the gift of God is eternal life through Jesus Christ our Lord." The Bible also reads, "For whosoever shall call upon the name of the Lord shall be saved." You are a "whosoever."

Lord, bless this person who is reading this right now and bless their family with long and healthy lives. Jesus, make Yourself real to them and do a quick work in their heart. If they have not received Jesus Christ as their Lord and Savior, I pray they will do so now in Jesus Name. Amen.

If you would like to receive the gift that God has for you today, say this out loud with your heart and lips.

"Dear Lord Jesus, come into my heart. Forgive me of my sins. Wash me and cleanse me. Set me free. Jesus, thank You that You died for me. I believe that You are risen from the dead and that You're coming back again for me. Fill me with the Holy Spirit. Give me a passion for the lost, a hunger for the things of

God and a holy boldness to preach the gospel of Jesus Christ. I'm saved; I'm born again, I'm forgiven and I'm on my way to Heaven because I have Jesus in my heart."

As a minister of the gospel of Jesus Christ, I tell you today that all of your sins are forgiven. Always remember to run to God and not from God because He loves you and has a great plan for your life.

Please find a church that believes the entire Bible and preaches the pure Word of God. Be sure to read your Bible every day, even if it is just a small amount. The Word washes you and helps you to grow and come to know Your Lord more and more. It is food for your spirit and it heals you, encourages you, lifts you up, and teaches you on your life journey.

All of heaven is having a great party of celebration over you right now, rejoicing over your entry into The Kingdom! I rejoice with them! God bless you – always.

Volume One

BIOGRAPHY

I was born in Madison Tennessee in 1964. We lived in a small house directly off of Neely's Bend Road.
I have a sister and (2) brothers, we were all stair steps with me being the oldest.

Since birth my dad left and my mother remarried and added (2) siblings to our family (sisters), and my dad had a son from a previous marriage. This gave me another brother.

I have been married 14 years to my husband, Tracy Howard Willhite.

So many things change in one's life and you can continue to read more in my second series titled "A Crying Heart". You will see that the choices we make in life are crucial and God tries to show and direct us in His way, but we seem to want it our way.

Throughout my life I know that being still and letting God have His way is awesome. The heartaches are less and things seem to turn out are much more pleasing and peaceful.

GOD IS GOOD… ALL THE TIME

Volume One

ISBN-13: 978-1497418240
ISBN-10: 1497418240

THE HOLY BIBLE, NEW INTERNATIONAL VERSION®, NIV® Copyright © 1973, 1978, 1984, 2011 by Biblica, Inc.®
Used by permission. All rights reserved worldwide.

Heart of My Heart Publishing Co., LLC
www.three-sheep.com

Volume One

Books by Tessa Marie Grisham Willhite

***A Child Looking for Love* –**
The book that brought Tessa healing and it can bring healing to you too

Coming Soon

A Crying Heart

Made in the USA
San Bernardino, CA
28 March 2014